# YOUR KNOWLEDGE HAS VALUE

- We will publish your bachelor's and master's thesis, essays and papers

- Your own eBook and book - sold worldwide in all relevant shops

- Earn money with each sale

Upload your text at www.GRIN.com
and publish for free

Gebhard Deißler

# US-North Korean Strategic Intercultural Communication Simulation

## An Intercultural Experiential Learning Set

GRIN Publishing

**Bibliographic information published by the German National Library:**

The German National Library lists this publication in the National Bibliography; detailed bibliographic data are available on the Internet at http://dnb.dnb.de .

**Imprint:**

Copyright © 2013 GRIN Verlag, Open Publishing GmbH
Print and binding: Books on Demand GmbH, Norderstedt Germany
ISBN: 978-3-656-56681-6

**This book at GRIN:**

http://www.grin.com/en/e-book/213084/us-north-korean-strategic-intercultural-communication-simulation

**GRIN - Your knowledge has value**

Since its foundation in 1998, GRIN has specialized in publishing academic texts by students, college teachers and other academics as e-book and printed book. The website www.grin.com is an ideal platform for presenting term papers, final papers, scientific essays, dissertations and specialist books.

**Visit us on the internet:**

http://www.grin.com/

http://www.facebook.com/grincom

http://www.twitter.com/grin_com

## *Transcultural Management*

Gebhard Deißler D.E.A./UNIV. PARIS I

# US-NORTH KOREA STRATEGIC INTERCULTURAL COMMUNICATION SIMULATION

# AN INTERCULTURAL EXPERIENTIAL LEARNING SET

CULTURE   RESEARCH

KULTUR FORSCHUNG

RECHERCHE CULTURE

BÚSQUEDA CULTURAL

RICERCA   CULTURALE

跨文化的智慧精髓

Uтранскультурная

Interkulturelles- u. Transkulturelles Management (German)

Intercultural &Transcultural Management (English)

Gestion Interculturelle et Gestion Transculturelle (French)

Gerencia Intercultural y Gerencia Transcultural (Spanish)

Gerência Intercultural e Gerência Transcultural (Portuguese)

跨文化的智慧精髓 - kua wen hua de zhi hui jing sui (Chinese)

транскультурная компетенция - transkulturnaja kompetencija (Russian)

toransukaruchā ・ manējimento (Japanese)

トランスカルチャー ・ マネジメント

Vishua Chaytana (Sanskrit)

# Index

4

# A Strategic Intercultural Simulation (Experiential Learning)

# The US Versus North Korea, A Topical Bilateral Interfacing of Societal/Political Cultures

# A highly participative group activity, aimed at developing and enhancing CQ – cultural intelligence

The following was a hand-out to international business students in the context of the subject Intercultural Relations and Communication of October 2006 designed to develop intercultural sensitivity and skills through the exploration of US – Korean intercultural relations. As one can see, the question has not been solved to this day. On the contrary, presently, North Korea is threatening the world with nuclear war.

Due to the importance of it I have decided to make this intercultural experiential learning set available to international/intercultural educators and students in part 1, while part 2 contextualizes the intercultural challenge in a transcultural approach.

In line with Richard D. Lewis one may assume that ..."in terms of deeply rooted culture, all Koreans are the same." Luckily, one may be inclined to say, because reliable intercultural research data are, as far as I know, only available for South Korea. So, we ground the experiential learning set on the assumption of the identity of core beliefs. The differences in political structures may, however, have conditioned people in the North and the South of the ideologically divided to develop different world views in a context of political isolation with few allies.

In short, in the following intercultural research data for South Korea are used as a first approach to the issue to be nuanced by to the socio-political context of the North.

## Assignment

Planning of a hypothetical cultural interfacing (encounter) of North Korean and US delegations. With the help of the docent you should prepare a cultural analysis of the parties. For this purpose the plenum will be divided into two groups, a US and a North Korean delegation, who will meet after the preparation phase. The scope of the exercise will depend on the orientation and on the preparedness of the students.

## Strategic guideline

Sun Tzu's strategic principle paraphrased as follows: "If you don't know yourself, you never win, if you know yourself, you win sometimes, sometimes you lose, if you know yourself and your opponent, you will be victorious in a hundred battles."

**Culture profiles of the parties based on Geert Hofstede, Fons Trompenaars and Charles Hampden-Turner, Edward T. Hall and Richard D. Lewis:**

| **US values** | **VS** | **North Korean values** |
|---|---|---|
| Low context | | High context |
| (Communication style, space, time, information flow | | |
| Achievement culture | | Ascription culture |
| Referee government | | Coach government |
| Pioneer | | Imitator |
| Inner-directed | | Outer directed |
| Confrontation | | Importance of harmony |
| Sequential | | Synchronic |
| Universalist | | Particularist |
| Specific | | Diffuse |
| Individualist | | Collectivist |
| Lower power distance | | Higher power distance |
| Higher masculinity | | Lower masculinity |
| Low uncertainty avoidance | | Strong uncertainty avoidance |
| Short term orientation | | Long term orientation |

Importance of Kibun (face) and Hahn ("pent-up energies and frustration, that developed in the Korean psyche under conditions of extreme hardship and oppression." (R. D. Lewis in "When Cultures Collide", Chap. 58, p. 502)

**Korean cultural values according to Richard D. Lewis, "When Cultures collide – Leading Across Cultures", page 503:**

"Confucian ethic,

Vertical society,

Observance of protocol,

Toughness, creativity,

Tendency towards violence,

Nationalism,

Protection of kibun (inner feelings),

Respect for elders,

Competitive spirit,

Obsession with survival,

Adaptability,

Suspicion of neighbours,

Dislike of foreigners,

 Willingness to suffer hardship for the good of the country."

# Confucianism (from Transcultural Management Dictionary, G. Deißler, Grin-Verlag 2009)

| Konfuzianismus | Confucianism |
|---|---|
| Konfuzianismus und Maoismus wurden beide vom Zentrum der Macht heruntergereicht. Das Machtmotiv in Form großer Machtdistanz in verschiedener Ausprägung im zwischenmenschlichen und staatlichen Bereich ist ein zeitloses kulturelles Muster des Landes der Mitte. | Confucianism and Maoism were both imposed from the centre of power, in line with Chinese imperial tradition. The power motive in diverse configurations is a historical pattern and suggests cultural continuity of centralised authority. |
| **Konfuzius** | **Confucius** |
| Oder Meister Kong, Latinisierung von Kong Tze oder Kong fuzi, der als chinesischer Moralist und Logiker von 551 bis 479 v. Chr. lebte. Seine kulturelle Bedeutung: Obwohl der Architekt der nationalen Einheit Chinas, der chinesische Kaiser Tsin Che Huang Ti den Konfuzianismus auszumerzen suchte, herrscht die mit diesem ethischen System einhergehende Weltanschauung heutzutage nicht nur in China, sondern in großen Teilen Ostasien dermaßen vor, dass man jene Kulturen als konfuzianische Kulturen bezeichnen kann. Auch Mao Zedong betrachtete den Konfuzianismus als ursächlich für die Rückständigkeit Chinas, konnte ihn aber ebensowenig ausmerzen. Er gründet auf als wu lun (fünf grundlegende Beziehungen) bezeichneten traditionellen Werten, die durch die Fürsorge des Seniorpartners und die Loyalität des Juniorpartners gekennzeichnet sind und die Basis aller menschlichen Beziehungen bilden, sowie auf Geboten für die rechte Lebensweise. . | Or Master Kong, Roman transliteration of Kong Tze or Kong fuzi, Chinese moralist and logician who lived from 551 to 479 BC. His legacy: Although the Chinese emperor Tsin Che Huang Ti, the architect of Chinese national unity tried to eradicate Confucianism completely in 213 BC, the world view connected to his code of ethics survives to this day, not only in China but across East Asia, to such an extent that they can be called Confucian cultures. Mao Zedong as well considered it responsible for the backwardness of China, but could not eliminate it. It is indeed based on traditional values called the wu lun, i.e. unequal relationships characterized by a trade-off between seniors' care and juniors' loyalty governing all human relationships, as well as on precepts for the right way to live. |

| | Hofstede's LTO-dimension had been identified originally as Confucian Dynamism by Bond's Chinese Value Survey. |
| --- | --- |

## Key terms

NPT (non-proliferation treaty), WMD (weapons of mass destruction), Kibun and Hahn, denuclearization, negotiation strategy, envoy, intermediary, bilateral, multilateral talks, UN, Security Council, zero/non-zero sum game, values…

## Some questions to be reflected upon

How may these South Korean cultural value preferences be impacted by North Korean ideology and its political culture in the context of isolation?

What is the impact of culture on the interfacing?

What face saving devices should be considered to bring the parties back to the bilateral/multilateral negotiation table?

Who should take the initiative and why?

What are the stakes and the strategic objectives and power balance issues regionally and globally?

Decision-making styles?

Relevance of trust and trust building. How can it be built?

Considering the process as a whole, specify the most critical moment and explain it in strategic terms.

What could be the impact of a facilitator on the process as a whole?

Can you comment on the connection between North and South Korean culture in North-East Asian culture setting (culturally, historically, economically, strategically and ideologically?

What (other) questions are relevant? (Brainstorming)

## The Process of the experiential learning set

Once the delegations have done their preparatory word separately, the delegations should meet and enact an encounter. Depending on the availability of time delegation members may read the chapters on the two national cultures by R. D. Lewis, in particular the passages on negotiation behaviour. The simulation will then be debriefed in the plenum. The process as a whole has to be customized by needs.

# Bibliography

Adler, N (2002*) International Dimensions of Organizational Behavior*, South-Western, Cincinnati, Oh. ISBN: 0-324-05786-5

Apfelthaler, G (2002) *Interkulturelles Management: Die Bewältigung interkultureller Differenzen in der internationalen Unternehmenstätigkeit.* Manz, Wien

Audia, PG and Tams, S (2002) 'Goal Setting, Performance Appraisal, Feedback' in Gannon, M J and Newman, L (Eds.) *The Blackwell Handbook of Cross-Cultural Management*, Blackwell Publishers, Oxford. ISBN: 0-631-21430-5

Bartlett, CH and Ghoshal, S and Birkinshaw, J (2003) *Transnational Management. Text, Cases, and Readings in Cross-Border Management*, International Edition, McGraw-Hill/Irwine, New York, NY. ISBN: 007-123228-1

Belbin (1996) *Team Roles at Work*. Butterworth-Heinemann

Blackman C (1997) *Negotiating China. Case Studies and Strategies*, St. Leonards, NWS, AUS. ISBN: 186448070X

Bond (1988) *The Cross-Cultural Challenge to Social Psychology*. Books on Demand.

Brannen MY and Salk JE (2000) Partnering Across Borders: Negotiating organizational culture in a German-Japanese joint venture, *Human Relations*, Volume 53(4) 451- 487, Sage Publications, London

Brosse, T (1984). *La Conscience-Energie. Structure de l'Homme et de l'Univers. Ses implications scientifiques, sociales et spirituelles.* Editions Présence. Sisteron. ISBN 2-901696-15-5

Davison, S C, Ward K (1999) *Leading International Teams.* McGraw-Hill. Maidenhead. ISBN: 0 07 709209 4.

Delahaye, Y (1977) *La Frontière Et Le Texte,* Payot, Paris. ISBN: 2-228-11850-09

Ewington, N (2004) *Workbook Unit 1, Workbook unit 2 and Workbook Unit 3,* CPI University of Cambridge, UK

Fisher G (1993) *International Negotiations. A Cross-Cultural Perspective.* Intercultural Press, Yarmouth, Maine. ISBN: 0-8039-4051-3

Ghemawat, P (2001) Distance Still Matters. The Hard Reality of Global Expansion. *Harvard Business Review.* September 2001

Goodall, K and Roberts, J (2003) Repairing Managerial Knowledge-Ability over Distance. Organisation Studies 24 (7): 1153 – 1175, Sage Publications, London

Goodall, K and Roberts, J (2003) Only connect: teamwork in the multinational. *Journal of World Business* 38 (2003) 150-164, Pergamon

Goodall, K (2002) Managing to Learn: from cross-cultural theory to education practice, Warner M and Joynt P (Eds.) *Managing Across Cultures: Issues and Perspectives.* Thompson Learning

Govindarajan, V and Gupta A K (2001) Building an Effective Global Business Team, *MIT Sloan Management Review,* Summer 2001

Hampden-Turner, Ch and Trompenaars, F (2002) *Building Cross-Cultural Competence. How to create wealth from conflicting values,* John Wiley and Sons Ltd, Chichester, England. ISBN: 0-471-49527-1

Hall, E (1990) *Beyond Culture.* Anchor

Hersey, P and Blanchard, K H (1993) *Management of Organizational Behaviour: Utilizing Human Resources, 6th edition,* Prentice Hall

Hickson, DJ and Pugh, DS (2001) *Management Worldwide. Distinctive Styles Amid Globalization*, Penguin Books Ltd, London. ISBN: 0-14100603-X.

Hodgetts, R M and Luthans, F (2003): *International Management: culture, strategy, and behaviour*, Boston, Mass., McGraw-Hill

Hofstede, G (1980) *Culture's Consequences, International Differences in Work-Related Values*, Sage Publications, Newbury Park, Ca. ISBN: 0-8039-1444-

Hofstede, G (2002) *Cultures and Organizations. Intercultural Cooperation and its Importance for Survival. Software of the Mind*, Profile Books Ltd, London. ISBN: 1-86197-543-

Hofstede, G (2003) *Culture and Organizations. Intercultural Cooperation and its Importance for Survival, Software of the Mind, Profile Books Ltd, London*. ISBN: 1 8697 543 0

Hofstede, G and Hofstede, G J (2005) *Culture and Organizations. Intercultural Cooperation and its Importance for Survival, Software of the Mind*, McGraw-Hill: ISBN: 0-07-143959-5

Holden, N (2004) *German as a Language of Management: Pragmatic Observations of German-style Networking and Knowledge-Sharing*, Interknow Workshop II, Regensburg.

Knapp, K (1996) 'Interpersonale und interkulturelle Kommunikation' in Bergemann, N (Ed.) *Interkulturelle Kommunikation*, Physica-Verlag, Heidelberg. ISBN: 3-7908-0913-6

Lax D A and Sebenius J K (2003) '3-D Negotiations. Playing the Whole Game' in Harvard Business Review, pp Nov. 03. ISSN

Krishnamurti, Jiddu. Various Talks across the world. Personal attendance.

Maisonrouge J (1988) *Inside IBM. A European's Story*. Collins. London. ISBN: 0-00-217692-0

Mole, J (1993) *Mind your Manners. Managing Culture Clash in the Single European Market*, Industrial Society Press, London. ISBN: 1 85788 000 5

Mullins, L J (2002) *Management and Organisational Behaviour, 6th edition*, Prentice Hall

Naipaul V S. (1984) *Finding the Centre*, Penguin Books Ltd. Harmondsworth, Middlesex, England

14

Price, S (2000) 'A View from a Bridge: Stereotypes of the German in Business and
Higher Education' in Emig, R (Ed.) Stereotypes in Contemporary Anglo-German
Relations', Macmillan Press Ltd, Basingstoke. ISBN: 0-333-79341-2

Steers, R and Sanchez-Runde, C (2002) 'Culture, Motivation, and Work Bahavior' in
Gannon, M J and Newman, K L (Eds.) *The Blackwell Handbook of Cross-Cultural
Management, Blackwell Publishers,* Oxford. ISBN: 0-631-21430-5

Singh, D  Talks across the World. Personal listening

Singh, R  Talks and Conferences. Personal attendance

Stuart, R and Barsoux, JL and  Kieser, A and Ganter, HD and Wagenbach, P (1994)
*Managing in Britain and in Germany,* The Macmillan Press Ltd, Basingstoke.
ISBN: 0-312-12237-3

Triandis, H C (2002) 'Generic Individualism and Collectivism' in Gannon, M J and
Newman, KL (Eds.) *The Blackwell Handbook of Cross-Cultural Management,*
Blackwell Publishers Ltd, Oxford. ISBN: 0-631-21430-5

Tsuda, I Personal Acquaintance and Cahiers de Tsuda

Weidenfeld, G (1999) "Englisches Deutschlandbild" in *Die Politische Meinung,* Volume  358,
Nr.10, pp 55-62. ISSN: 00323446.

Yong, L and Kammhuber, S (2003) 'Ostasien: China' (East-Asia: China) in Thomas, A and
Kinast, U and Schroll-Machl, S (Eds.) *Handbuch der Internationalen Kommunikation und
Kooperation, Band 1. (Handbook of International Communication and Cooperation, Volume
1)* Vandenhoeck & Ruprecht, Goettingen. ISBN: 3-525-46172-0.

Worldwork (2002) *International Management Development. The International Profiler,*
London

**"When remedies are past, the griefs are ended."**


(William Shakespeare)


"Neither are remedies past nor are the griefs ended", we might paraphrase Shakespeare, but if we do not use the communication and negotiation remedy at its best, the griefs might still be coming.